Sea Turtles

Laura Marsh

NATIONAL GEOGRAPHIC

Washington, D.C.

For Eliza
—L. F. M.

Design by Yay Design

Paperback ISBN: 978-1-4263-0853-6
Hardcover ISBN: 978-1-4263-0854-3

cover, Masa Ushioda/www.coolwaterphoto.com; 1, Carson Ganci/Design Pics/Corbis; 2, Frans Lanting/
NationalGeographicStock.com; 4-5, Aquascopic/Alamy; 6-7, Jason Isley, Scubazoo/Getty Images; 8, Jason
Isley, Scubazoo/Getty Images; 10, Image Quest Marine; 11 (top), Doug Perrine/SeaPics.com; 11 (bottom), Luiz
Claudio Marigo/naturepl.com; 12 (top), James D. Watt/SeaPics.com; 12 (bottom), George Burba/Shutterstock;
13 (top), Doug Perrine/SeaPics.com; 13 (bottom), Image Quest Marine; 14, Doug Perrine/naturepl.com; 15,
Mitsuaki Iwago/Minden Pictures; 16, Wild Wonders of Europe/Zankl/naturepl.com; 18, Jason Bradley; 20,
Doug Perrine/naturepl.com; 21, Frans Lemmens/Getty Images; 22, Luciano Candisani/Minden Pictures; 23
(top), Nils Bornemann/iStockphoto.com; 23 (bottom), Norbert Wu/Getty Images; 24, Jeffrey L. Rotman/Cor-
bis; 25, Jim Richardson/NationalGeographicStock.com; 26, Julie Dermansky/Corbis; 27, 28, 29 (top), Audubon
Nature Institute, New Orleans; 29 (bottom), Heather Stanley, Audubon Nature Institute, New Orleans; 30
(top), Frank and Helena/Getty Images; 30 (bottom), Gorilla/Shutterstock; 31 (top), hardcoreboy/iStockphoto.
com; 31 (center), Stacie Stauff Smith Photography/Shutterstock; 31 (bottom), Tim Platt/Getty Images; 32 (top
left), Vlue/Shutterstock; 32 (top right), Doug Perrine/SeaPics.com; 32 (left center), Wild Wonders of Europe/
Zankl/naturepl.com; 32 (right center), Mitsuaki Iwago/Minden Pictures; 32 (bottom left), Stephen Frink/Getty
Images; 32 (bottom right), Jason Isley, Scubazoo/Getty Images

Printed in the United States of America
11/WOR/1

Table of Contents

A Sea Turtle!

Green sea turtle

What hatches on land but spends its life in the sea?

What starts out the size of a Ping-Pong ball but can grow up to seven feet long?

A sea turtle!

Ocean World

Leatherback sea turtle

Sea turtles are graceful swimmers in the water. Their flippers move like wings.

Turtle Term

REPTILE: A cold-blooded animal that lays eggs and has a backbone and scaly skin

Sea turtles travel the world in warm ocean waters. They are one of the few reptiles that live in the sea.

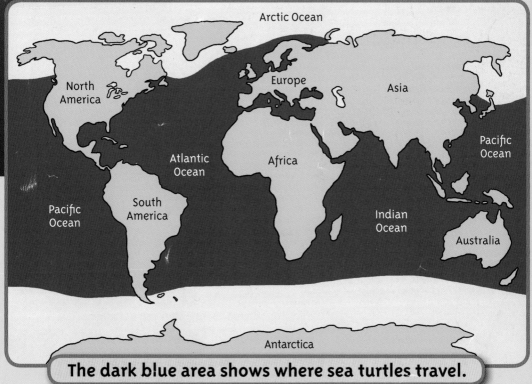

Arctic Ocean

North America

Europe

Asia

Atlantic Ocean

Africa

Pacific Ocean

Pacific Ocean

South America

Indian Ocean

Australia

Antarctica

The dark blue area shows where sea turtles travel.

A sleek body helps
the turtle move easily
through the water.

The scales
on its shell are
called scutes.

The back flippers steer
the turtle as it swims.
They are also used to
dig nests in the sand.

Green sea turtle

A sea turtle has lungs because it breathes air. A sea turtle holds its breath underwater.

Sea turtles can't pull their heads and limbs into their shells like land turtles can.

Their large, powerful flippers act like paddles.

Scientists believe some sea turtles live 80 years or more, but they don't know for sure.

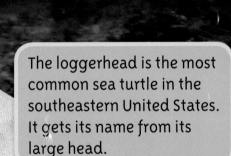

The loggerhead is the most common sea turtle in the southeastern United States. It gets its name from its large head.

There are seven kinds of sea turtles in the world. Each has special features.

The flatback has a flat body. It's the only sea turtle that doesn't live in U.S. waters. It lives near Australia.

The olive ridley has an olive-colored shell. It is shaped like a heart.

The hawksbill can't dive deep. It spends most of its time on the water's surface.

The green turtle has a small head. Unlike other sea turtles, it goes ashore to warm itself in the sun.

The Kemp's ridley likes shallow waters. It's the world's most endangered sea turtle.

Turtle Term

ENDANGERED: At risk of dying out

The leatherback doesn't have a hard shell. Its skin is rubbery with small bones underneath.

Nestbuilding

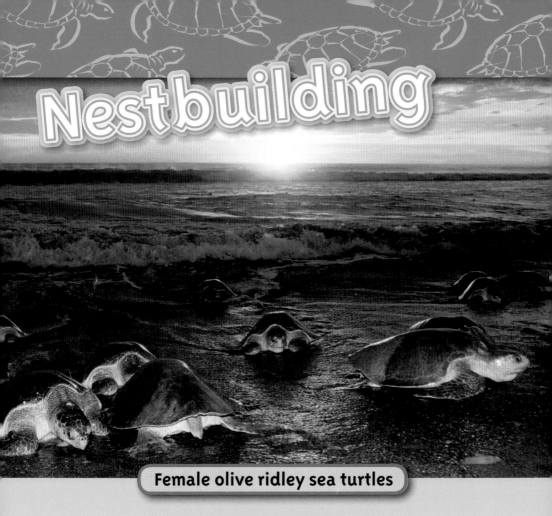

Female olive ridley sea turtles

A female sea turtle comes on land to lay her eggs. She usually returns to the same beach where she hatched.

Scientists aren't sure how sea turtles know where to go. They think sea turtles know by instinct.

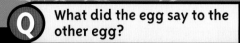
The sea turtle digs a hole with her back flippers. She lays her eggs and covers them with sand. Then she returns to the sea.

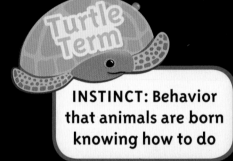

Turtle Term

INSTINCT: Behavior that animals are born knowing how to do

Female green sea turtle

15

Oh, Baby!

CRAAACK! The eggs hatch after 50 to 70 days. Tiny turtles called hatchlings crawl out of their eggshells.

Turtle Term

HATCHLING: A young animal that has just come out of its egg

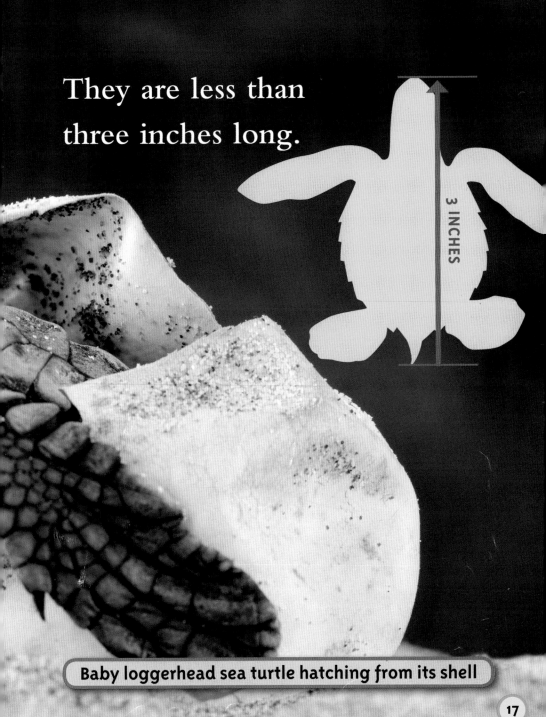

They are less than three inches long.

3 INCHES

Baby loggerhead sea turtle hatching from its shell

Hatchlings usually crawl toward the sea at night. In the dark, they are hidden from predators.

The little turtles follow the brightest light. The line where the sky meets the sea is the brightest natural light on a beach.

If the hatchlings follow this light, they will make it to the sea.

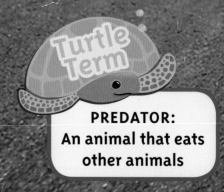

Turtle Term

PREDATOR:
An animal that eats other animals

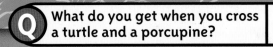

Q What do you get when you cross a turtle and a porcupine?

A A slowpoke!

Leatherback hatchling

Big and Small

The smallest sea turtles are the Kemp's ridley and the olive ridley. Adults are about two feet long and weigh up to 100 pounds.

Kemp's ridley sea turtle

Leatherback sea turtle

The largest sea turtle is the
Leatherback. It can grow up to
seven feet long and weigh more
than 2,000 pounds. That's about
ten men put together!

On the Menu

Green sea turtle

Munch, munch, what's for lunch?

Most sea turtles eat plants and animals. They dine on algae (AL-gee) and sea grasses. They also munch on crab and conchs.

Turtle Term

ALGAE: Simple, non-flowering plants that do not have stems, roots, or leaves

Jellyfish are a favorite food for many sea turtles. But plastic trash can look like jellyfish in the ocean, and that spells trouble! Swallowing trash can hurt and even kill sea turtles.

Green sea turtle

Danger!

Hawksbill sea turtle caught in a net

Trash isn't the only danger to sea turtles. Fishing nets and hungry animals can harm them, too.

Building lights confuse hatchlings so they don't reach the sea.

Leatherback sea turtle confused by city lights

Sometimes people even step on sea turtle nests by accident.

Sea Turtle Rescue

In 2010 a giant oil spill leaked into the Gulf of Mexico. Oil covered sea animals and washed up on beaches. Oil is dangerous to people and wildlife.

Oil on beaches in Louisiana

Oil-covered Kemp's ridley

People in charge of a sea turtle rescue program in Louisiana saved many sea turtles.

The rescuers cleaned the turtles and gave them medicine. People cared for them until they could return to the sea.

Kemp's ridley sea turtle

Safekeeping

You don't need to work at a sea turtle hospital to help sea turtles. Here are a few things you can do to keep them safe.

1

Pick up trash on the beach.

2

Don't release balloons into the air. (They often end up in the sea.)

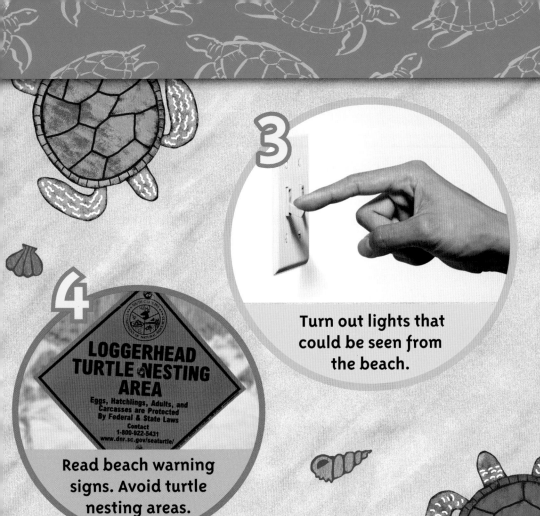

3

Turn out lights that could be seen from the beach.

4

LOGGERHEAD TURTLE NESTING AREA

Eggs, Hatchlings, Adults, and Carcasses are Protected By Federal & State Laws
Contact
1-800-922-5431
www.dnr.sc.gov/seaturtle/

Read beach warning signs. Avoid turtle nesting areas.

5

Tell your classmates what you've learned about sea turtles.

Glossary

ALGAE: Simple, non-flowering plants that do not have stems, roots, or leaves

ENDANGERED: At risk of dying out

HATCHLING: A young animal that has just come out of its egg

INSTINCT: Behavior that animals are born knowing how to do

PREDATOR: An animal that eats other animals

REPTILE: A cold-blooded animal that lays eggs and has a backbone and scaly skin